MELBOURNE COVID LOCKDOWN PROTESTS

MELBOURNE COVID LOCKDOWN PROTESTS

Ash Jackson

Also Available from the Author:
"BEYOND TRANS"
ISBN: 9780975654613

Discover the riveting life journey of Ash Jackson, an award-winning musician who turned her pain into powerful music. From her childhood dreams of fame, struggles with self-esteem, and experiences of bullying, to her pro wrestling career, battles with mental health, and remarkable courage in navigating her gender affirmation, her story is one of resilience, self-discovery, and redemption. Ash's music is more than an expression of art; it is a raw portrayal of her life, encapsulating themes of loneliness, love, and trauma. Yet, Ash's life is not solely confined to the realm of music. Her involvement in the anti-lockdown movement in Melbourne, and her subsequent defection and fallout are just some episodes of her multi-faceted tale

Further information can be found at.
www.ashjackson.com

Copyright © 2024 by Ash Jackson

All rights reserved. No part of this book may be reproduced in any manner whatsoever without written permission except in the case of brief quotations embodied in critical articles and reviews.

First Printing, 2024

Preface

As the author of this booklet I thought it would be appropriate to introduce myself in context to the events proceeding herein. At the time of Covid-19 I was in my late forties and several years into the process of my gender transition from being born as a male to living full-time as a woman. You can read more about my gender journey in my autobiography "Beyond Trans" where I go into much more detail.

I am releasing my story not as a vindictive revenge plot, but simply to inform the general public of what went on behind-the-scenes of the protest movement in Melbourne during that time. I have no ill-will against anyone mentioned in this story, but it was written at a time when I was still quite a mess, and so for sake of authenticity, I release it now with warts and all without any fear of retribution or litigation. After all this is what happened...

1

Covid & Protests

In March 2020, the world braced itself for the COVID-19 pandemic. Over the next few months things began to close due to government restrictions and eventually curfews. It couldn't have been worse timing for me. I had received a public liability payout from my knee injury and it would have been enough to pay for my gender reassignment surgery. Well, now that the world was in lockdown that wasn't going to happen so my loneliness was compensated by splurging on music equipment that I had never been able to afford previously.

As the last month approached until I would have to find a new home, I began getting deeply entrenched in researching COVID-19 and became exposed to the multiple websites and Facebook groups discussing the once-in-a-century plaque. I had way too much time on my hands and anger that my life-changing plans were being wiped out because of my solitude. I moved to St Kilda the weekend of the Dan Andrews (Victorian Premier) announcement of a six-week stay-at-home order and night-time curfew. I was about to slip into a giant rabbit hole that would consume my entire life and send me into a collision course with authorities.

What do you do when you cannot leave a room? You leave it anyway and hope you don't get caught which I did dozens of times, but it's the mental anguish that started to do my head in. I started researching conspiracy theories and joined multiple chat rooms on the encrypted phone app called Telegram where I would regularly speak with Morgan Jonas, Monica Smit, Steve Booth (aka Schteve Riley), Matt Lawson, Mel Ann and Bren Edgerton.

My days became consumed with "research" and believing eventually that the COVID "scam" was nothing more than the worldwide governments forming a police state, where we would be sent to concentration camps if we did not participate in compliance. After seeing Victoria Police manhandle so many hundreds of protestors online while I watched the live streams, I began to think of them as a version of the Gestapo. It sounds crazy writing this but that is what I truly believed and I was ready to join the cause at a higher level and fight for our lost freedom.

My first anti-mask/anti-lockdown protest was in October of 2020 and I made up fake credentials as a journalist complete with a legal sole-trader work permit, ID badge and the good old handycam from my Oz Fish TV filming days. It started around the Shrine of Remembrance and the police and protesters became extremely violent with each other. I would later find out it was the "Proud Boys" crew that were the ones trading punches with police. I followed the rest of the peaceful protesters on their walk to the bridge just before the Yarra River and Flinders Street station. I ended up on channel 7 news that night, the first of many times, with me pretending I was a journalist (face mask intact) and filming a scuffle between police and some old guy on the front line as they brought things back to order.

I felt sorry for the officers being a metre or so away, as they were mostly very young and you could see a sense of fear in their eyes, knowing that this could turn very bad at any moment if the thousands-strong crowd decided to break their line. My life now was 100% consumed with the COVID pandemic (or as we all called it "just a more severe case of the flu") and the harsh restrictions with growing distaste for the police. My sanity was being tested profoundly as I spent two months without any human contact while my paranoia and hatred towards those enforcing these restrictions increased to the point of planned suicidal thoughts. If I did not find a community I would have taken my life as a lot of people did during that time.

I found that community online and they had all become my new family. I attended all the other protests in the following months but it wasn't until February of 2021, when I met all these leaders in person at a snap-protest on Thursday the 18th at Flinders Street, that I became much more heavily involved and had nothing but utter contempt for the government, the police, Premier Dan Andrews and the mainstream media.

That night was a magical evening. I met Mel Ann at Flinders Street station and waited for the crowd to arrive. Dan Andrews had announced a strict lockdown again and as always we had a 7pm protest planned on any occasion that he announced such a quick shut down. I had called live on air to Tom Elliot at 3AW and invited his listeners to come and join us and his response was "I wouldn't recommend that because protesting is illegal during COVID restrictions".

That night around two thousand of us marched from Flinders Street to Rod Laver Arena as a show against the tennis being allowed to keep going while we were all locked up. Then it was a long walk back to Parliament House where I met up with Monica Smit and became her camera operator for the rest of the night. I also got to chat and march alongside Steve Booth (online name Schteve Riley) while he carried his enormous flag pole displaying the countries of England, the United States and of course Australia.

While the speeches started at the steps of Parliament, protected by about fifty police officers, an older guy named Bren sang a song called "We Are Coming" that he had written. I introduced myself as a fellow musician and suggested he record that song with a full band sound. He was a bit dismissive as he had just met me but within a couple of months, it was another successful collaboration and recording session.

I had no idea at the time that the protest movement I was involved with was mainly right-wing, but it was something I would discover in the ensuing months as I climbed my way up the ladder as a front-runner for each protest always making it on the national news on television and in the newspapers. One particular aspect of the right-wing involvement was run by a silly pseudo-religious group called the "Australian Peacemakers", run at that time by Nick Patterson and neo-nazi Jarrod "Jaz" Searby among others. They were just starting to make a tiny baby imprint on the leadership of the movement and it got me a little bit concerned as I knew that we were an anti-LGBT group with links to their original involvement with the "Proud Boys".

These people are a million percent on the ASIO watch list and some of their associate colleagues include Neil Erikson Tom Sewell and Blair Cottrell. Three very extreme neo-nazis that would love nothing more than to bash the hell out of me or any trans person, but I kept getting most of the press and I imagine that pissed them off. A transgender woman keeps getting the majority of pics in the newspapers and film footage on the nightly news. I guess diversity can have its positive spin although looking back I think they let me march out front of the protests to dispel allegations of being right-wing bigots.

I imagine their train of thought must have been "No we don't discriminate, have a look at Ash out front carrying Schteve's three-flag pole". I didn't carry that pole until a week later but keep reading, the story has a while to go to fill you in on the events of the next week, which would involve serious illegal activity, imprisonment for someone and weeks of paranoia for me barricading my home with booby-traps and waiting for police and ASIO to knock my door down. This is how brainwashing for a belief works, you can seriously justify anything, perhaps even murder if what you believe is perceived as your truth. Absolutely anything, hence why a terrorist feels zero guilt for killing others. They believe they are in the right.

That is what it feels like to be brainwashed...

On Saturday, February 20th, 2021 a protest was set for Fawkner Park which was about a ten-minute tram ride from where I was living in at the time. I got up later in the morning, had a few shots of vodka (aka liquid courage) and got ready as it was forecast to be a very warm day. Put a summer dress and sandals on (a big mistake if I knew how much walking I would be doing in the following hours) and chucked a vodka flask, purse, keys and Ventolin.

I remember rocking up there and quickly saying hi to Monica, Mel Ann and Raph Fernandez before deliberately obscuring the camera view of all the mainstream media by standing in front of their long lenses and moving once they did. it was like a game of baby chess for the next hour and I knew I had pissed them off in a major way. One even came up asking me to move and I pretended to talk in some pseudo-asian language not being able to understand just for my personal amusement in annoying him.

Member of Parliament Catherine Cummings did the first speech but got booed off the stage for asking us all to "socially distance" or the police would stop the gathering. There were hundreds of police already showing signs of kettling which is where they surround a group and pick them out violently one by one. The process had been used before on last year's Melbourne Cup Day in the city near the Parliament building. I was lucky I was sick that day so I didn't go, but the process of kettling and arresting each person on that particular day took many hours in the hot sun, with police not allowing anyone to even go to the toilet or access to water.

Monica gave a very emotional speech that day and I was very moved by her statement that she was willing to die for the cause. Then the storm troopers came in while people ran out to the main road led by Schteve with his flag pole. I tried my best to catch up but they were too far ahead. Once we turned the corner the police had completely barricaded any further access, so we had to turn back and return to Faulkner Park where reporters were running around trying to get their story for that night's news.

Police had set up another blockade so we were almost completely kettled in. I walked up to them feeling brave and tried to get through, then foolishly tried to perform a citizen's arrest on them. I was instantly put into handcuffs and I asked them to go easy because of my tendinitis wrist issues, but all it made them do was tighten them so my hands became numb. I was taken over to the booking area and I refused a search or to give my name. The group of male cops sitting and resting looked like something from a future science-fiction army and they were giggling at me. I was nothing but a guy in a dress to them and my rage resulted in me calling them every swear word you could ever imagine with zero fear of charges or detention. Eventually, I gave them my name so I could get released pending a possible five thousand dollar fine in the mail.

I went back in, getting in the police's faces again, right up the front line near Schteve as he called them "Nazi dogs". The police had lost their kettle line and you could see panic in the faces of the younger members. I even got kicked so hard in my calf that I could barely hobble as I walked off with Schteve to see him off to his car. What a day this had been and yes I was indeed on the national news that night, interviewed briefly by Channel 7 reporter Paul Dowsley.

Me at protests & being arrested again and again

The protest leaders

The next day started with an online chat with Schteve and he had a plan for that Sunday night during the Australian Open tennis final. The plan didn't work and I knew that it wouldn't succeed upon arriving to meet him outside of Rod Laver Arena, although we did get up to some illegal antics that night which police are very well aware of courtesy of me when I defected from the movement many months later. If his plan had worked it would have been worldwide news and something no one has ever done before, so I shall leave it at that.

A few days later Schteve was arrested by the terrorism division of the police for using a slingshot to smash the front office window of Dan Andrews. He had been on their radar now for months and he was caught because police recognised the distinctive style and colour of his shoes on CCTC footage. He was remanded in custody for about sixteen or so days and in solitary confinement because of COVID requirements. No one heard a thing from him for many months and I imagine that the stress of being alone in your thoughts and away from his wife and two young children would have left him a partially broken man.

On March 20th I attended another protest, this time at Treasury Gardens near Parliament House and the place was swarming with police. I said hello to Monica and Morgan while and Bren Edgerton got up to sing a couple of songs on his acoustic guitar with a sign attached to it saying "FREE SCHTEVE". I also had a decent chat with citizen journalist Avi Yemini and offered my services as a camera operator.

We exchanged numbers and listened to the speeches while the Victoria Police Intelligence Unit got good footage of every person there. I even was a smart-ass and tried to block their view with their pathetic handycam, which surprised me having a much bigger budget than I ever had while using one to film my television shows.

Catherine Cummings was there again and we had a chat. This time the police let the protest finish without interruption. About a week later another smaller protest was planned in front of Daniel Andrew's office and I got a call from Avi to help him out filming that night. Bren showed up carrying Schteve's three-flag pole and I thought that was such an honourable gesture. Avi's cameraman eventually showed up so I wasn't needed but I did help Monica and her father set up the portable stage but was feeling a bit left out and insecure being transgender, in what I was slowly discovering a mostly right-wing movement.

I met Catherine a few more times at a nightclub in Footscray and we would discuss the situation with lockdowns and Dan Andrews in great depth. My birthday was held there in late March and I was really surprised and happy that she also attended the "Pride of Our Footscray" club to celebrate with my other friends. "Pride" has always been a very safe and welcoming venue run by Mat O'Keefe and a lovely mixture of LGBT and straight people. When we all first started attending years before it was hard to fill the room with patrons but as I now sit here and write this I can assure and recommend to you the reader that it is now a world-class venue as a pub, cocktail bar and night club.

Around April of 2021, I put together some backing tracks with my limited home studio for two of Bren's songs. I thought they might become an anthem for any of the upcoming protests. His original song "We Are Coming" turned out well as a rock song with drums, bass, and guitar from myself. He also re-wrote the words to "I Was Only 19" by an Australian band called Redgum, but renamed it "Bullshit 19". I produced the video clips for each song with Bren in front of a green screen and various protest clips shown in the background courtesy of fellow protester Marty Focker and a political branch called "Reignite Democracy Australia" run by Monica.

The songs got some great feedback from the protest movement and I was proud to be involved as a higher-level participant now, but that was all about to change thanks to that fringe organisation calling themselves the "Australian Peacemakers". My last few days in the movement were filled with extreme hatred towards police and utter contempt for the draconian measures now about to ramp up to an extreme level again.

Leading up to these last few weeks of my involvement I had started writing a novel based on a future that I saw as controlled by authorities and those that disagreed had to form an underground movement to fight back, so basically the same as John Connor did in the "Terminator" movies. It started with a technical manual titled "Anti-Police Protest Tactics" or something like that. I eventually deleted all traces of it but it was a well-researched booklet with topics like fake ID, disguises, booby-traps, high-grade lasers, fishing hook snares, remote control offensives with drones, flares, a huge section on how to get out of a kettling situation and various booby-traps. It was on the verge of being a terrorist manual aimed against the police, but in my mind it was just part of my novel.

I still have trouble coming to terms with the fact I wrote something and I don't want to mention any other topics from it in case some true nutcase decides to fulfill their stupid cause and hurt people for real. It was a chapter in a fictional novel but I sent part of it to my cousin Rachael Gaylor because she was also a conspiracy theorist like me, but didn't realise that her partner Sam was a member of the Australian Peacemakers. It was a huge mistake as I would discover less than a week after finally deciding the movement was not for me. The Australian Peacemakers claimed they were doing God's work by defending any member of the public against police during weekly protests and they did not like me at all because I was transgender, an abomination as described in the Bible..

Leading up to the events of May 29th, 2021 I barely had heard their name but my cousin Rachael and I regularly got into mild arguments because she thought my role in the movement was minimal at best. It seemed like a massive jealousy ploy and it was strange because she was one of my only few cousins, out of many dozens, who regularly spoke with me and encouraged me with my transition journey. The Peacemakers despise all LGBT people and I was starting to see a similar twist in the values expressed by the anti-lockdown movement.

Thursday, May the 27th there was another snap-lockdown announced so again we all headed in our thousands to Flinders Street station for the ritual 7pm protest. By this point and actually for a couple of months now, I had been out front of the marches carrying an imitation three-flag pole in honor of Schteve. We ended up at Parliament House again but I kept hearing reports about Nick Patterson making threats to police online and even threatening them on that night. He would work in such a way as to appear macho but without advertising an obvious intention. Here are some of his quotes:

"You have the right to punch police officers in the face even if they don't detain you" (an online video conversation discussing the self-defense statute)

"Now we might be terrorising the powers that be if we get organised and according to them we could be terrorists...but that's good, we want them to be terrorised" (an online video conversation)

"If the police do the right thing, the government does the right thing, there's not going to be a problem" (speech at Batman Park May 15th)

"They want us to react, they want us to be violent. And I tell you I will be violent if I have to be" (speech at Flinders St May 27th)

"What you've done justifies our response that's coming because we have grounds for it now" (challenging police, May 29th in North Melbourne)

So Saturday, May the 29th arrived and the police warnings were getting full on. A protest was set for Flagstaff Gardens around midday but it was now 100% illegal to be five kilometres from your home and the cops were promoting it as a "ring of steel" around the area. I carried my three flag pole in honour of Schteve again, broken down in thirds as it was a surf fishing rod and I made my way to the gardens after getting off at Flagstaff station. I quickly attempted to set up my flag pole but I barely made it one hundred metres before the police stopped me. They wanted to know what I was doing and I refused to answer and used the traditional conspiracy-theorist round of asking each of them for their names and badge numbers. I still tried to push past the police but was restrained and threatened with arrest. There was a picture of it in the newspaper the next day courtesy of the Herald Sun. To be fair the cops took it very easy on me and gave me a move on order and upon realising I wouldn't be getting far that day, I left to try and find any fellow protesters in other locations. It wasn't long before I saw some others and they said they were meeting at a new location at the Queen Victoria Market so I ventured my way through the smaller lanes to the car park of the market.

I noticed one of the leaders of the protest Matt Lawson was there with about fifteen or so others. As I quickly assembled my flags I began walking towards the ensuing police unit that was walking sternly towards us from about 100 metres away. I was wondering why there was no chatting or for that matter any noise behind me. I turned around to realise they had all run off like cowards. A leader who had done speeches at rallies, organised and marshalled illegal protests, yet there he was scurrying off down a side street. I was in disbelief as I thought he was a stand-up guy, but then a light-bulb moment illuminated itself: I think I have been being used by this movement. I had been told they were mainly right-wing and possibly anti-LGBT but maybe they were letting me hang around so their defense could always be to critical journalists "We are LGBT friendly, see look at Ash on the frontline" as mentioned previously. Ironically less than two years later they were among those protesting their hatred towards transgender people alongside Posey Parker at Parliament House. Also there were the Peacemakers and Neo-Nazi crowd led by Tom Sewell who would love nothing more to wipe people like me from the planet.

While the officers questioned me I kind of "gave it all up" at that moment. I was so stunned at how I had been betrayed that I fully co-operated with the police as they gave me a new move-on order. I called Schteve on my way home but didn't mention where my head was at now. He told me a major incident had occurred not far from where I was involving the Peacemakers, saying the police had assaulted and pepper sprayed them. The Peacemakers had been taunting police at Flagstaff and Nick Patterson thought he was outsmarting police by referring to precedents for freedom of movement, not having to identify etc. He had forgotten one major point in his pseudo-law-expert argument: "There were COVID directives set out as law during these times and it disqualified all legal context he was trying to make". Finally, the police walked towards the group to stop them from progressing and Nick and his followers just ran straight at the cops and went at it with fists and of course lost, with Nick receiving a broken shoulder. A bit of advice for anyone out there: Do not run at the police especially after you have just yelled at them "What you've done justifies what we're going to do because we have grounds for it now".

Nick Patterson from "Peacemakers" doing God's peaceful work?!?!

Schteve had been watching a livestream Facebook feed from Raph Fernadez and said it looked pretty full on. That was my final interaction with Schteve. After I left the movement he would often post transphobic memes on social media like "The only difference between tyranny and a tranny is Y" (obviously meaning why) and as a deliberate dig at me after my defection.

A few days passed until the police came knocking again. This time they took me into custody temporarily and interviewed me about a conversation I had had with my cousin Rachael and I couldn't believe what I was reading and seeing. She had given a copy of my "booklet" to the police electronically and as they showed me parts from it I was shocked at how far I had fallen down the rabbit hole. Suddenly my most supportive cousin had written a statement referring to me as "he" and "him" and I knew her partner Sam from the Peacemakers was probably involved. There can be a lot of jealousy among those groups regarding media attention and she was probably annoyed that I kept getting in the newspapers as opposed to Sam, who was arrested alongside Nick Patterson for assaulting police. I was charged with various offences pending a court summons for indictable acts. I went home and my brain shut itself off as I spent many days in bed.

That Friday I got visited by two officers to hand me the usual letter warning me not to attend the forecasted protest the next day. I told them I had decided to leave that crazy cult and suddenly their stern looks turned into that of approval. An hour later I got a visit from two detectives concerned about the potential for violence tomorrow and I told them the same thing. Eventually I would correspond with them about some of the inner workings of the movement that I was still aware of.

The police officers who charged me taught me a valuable life lesson the prior few days before. They said, "Ash you are very intelligent, most of the people we deal with are not. You have a chance here to change and it's never too late". It finally dawned on me they were there to help me, their job was to help people and get them back into a life of not offending. It was funny how fast I had gone from being a cop hater to the realisation that they are mostly good people doing their job called law enforcement. They said they didn't necessarily want to go to the protests and also pointed out that there are bad apples in every line of work, but maybe I had been only watching the bad stuff portrayed on social media. I went home relieved. I had finally decided: I am done...

2

Anti-Scamming

Over the next few months I corresponded with a detective regarding issues and my knowledge of the "anti-everything" movement. Every couple of weeks I would get a visit from the officers that interviewed me to drop off paperwork, but more importantly they checked up on me to see how I was doing. That impressed me greatly and was the last nail in the coffin for me to 100% disassociate with that cult. If they didn't show that concern then I imagine I might have eventually started looking at conspiracy theories again and fell back down the hole.

The charges were all dropped once the case got to court about a year later and my cousin looked quite foolish as my lawyer tore apart her accusations as nothing more than a family squabble, all the while accusing me of things while sabotaging that by referring to me with deliberate incorrect pronouns and egging me on to reply to her so I looked like the bad one. The prosecutor who dropped all the charges wished me well and he hoped I was doing better. It was time to move on but we were still in COVID times so I temporarily moved back to my parents' home and began to heal from the effects of the brainwashing I had endured from by others, but mostly by myself...

By late June to early July, I was starting to heal a bit from the mental damage inflicted on me for such a fake cause. I kept hearing online about this guy that was intensely pissing off the people I had once stood with at protests and was calling them out for the scamming that they were doing, which I was very much unaware of. His name was "Lucky" Lance Simon and he had a sordid history himself, having been involved most of his life in crime and even acquitted of murder a decade or so prior, but had turned his life around and got married and had children. I thought I would visit his social media page and see what he had to say as all I heard previously from my prior cult days was how much he was hated and even rumours about exacting revenge on him.

I was quite surprised at how entertaining and charismatic he was in his videos. So I reached out and sent him a private message explaining that I used to be deep in the anti-everything movement, and he replied almost instantly asking if we could have a phone chat. We spoke for ages while I told him my story and over the next few weeks we became quite good friends, as I discovered how these people I once marched with had various ways of scamming followers out of thousands of dollars which combined would add up to many millions.

The basic principle of how they scam people is always through some interaction with the police. You record an incident where you are argumentative with them, trying to get a reaction that will offend them. Once charged by the police they then "grift" for legal fees way above what representation in court would cost. The term "grifting" means setting up a donation page, explaining the incident in their favour and asking for donations to fight the charge in court using a dodgy barrister who was probably in on it to begin with. Some would raise $50,000 to $200,000 for a matter that might cost $5000 at best and they pocket the rest.

Scam #2 is somewhat a bit more legitimate but still dodgy ethically. You film your interaction with police, drag the incident out and annoy them to the point that they have a somewhat entertaining edited video clip to post to a platform like YouTube. Then with monetization on the amount of views you get, which is roughly $10,000 per million views, you can make a nice paycheck. A lot of the people doing this, in particular Simeon Boikov (aka Aussie Cossack) became semi-famous in the movement but their egos would usually cause them to mess up and breach the terms of YouTube and eventually get banned. I think that moron is still in hiding at the Russian Embassy after he live-streamed himself assaulting an elderly man and a warrant issued for his arrest, probably delusionally thinking he is a now a political prisoner like Julian Assange.

Avi Yemini, another Melbourne based citizen journalist, is an expert at "grifting". I found some videos by commentator Tom Tanuki and Lucky Lance online demonstrating his attempts at convincing his followers to donate their hard-earned cash to him through a dodgy news outlet called "Rebel News" based in Canada with Yemini being the Australian correspondent. His campaigns to "fight the COVID fines" which took in hundreds of thousands of dollars, never required a lawyer to that amount, but pocketed the rest which is a standard scam in the grifting business.

On Australia Day a couple of years ago, he made a video live from the back of a police van claiming he was under arrest. This has been a main stable for Avi as he rocks up every year on that day to offend protesters and get footage of their sometimes awkward and hostile reactions. The police know him all too well and this year, similar to previous years, he was given nothing more than a move-on order. The police consider him more like a pest and usually put him in their van, dropping him off a few blocks away with that same move-on order again and the warning that if he comes back, he will be charged with disturbing the peace.

"I'm now in the back of a police car and I've been arrested for what they alledge is a breach of the peace. The breach was that I attended the so-called invasion day to report and do my job. I came with my federal accreditation from the government"

(It was actually a press pass only valid in Canberra for interviewing foreign political visitors)

The basic principle of how they scam people is always through some interaction with the police. You record an incident where you are argumentative with them, trying to get a reaction that will offend them. Once charged by the police they then "grift" for legal fees way above what representation in court would cost. The term "grifting" means setting up a donation page, explaining the incident in their favour and asking for donations to fight the charge in court using a dodgy barrister who was probably in on it to begin with. Some would raise $50,000 to $200,000 for a matter that might cost $5000 at best and they pocket the rest.

Scam #2 is somewhat a bit more legitimate but still dodgy ethically. You film your interaction with police, drag the incident out and annoy them to the point that they have a somewhat entertaining edited video clip to post to a platform like YouTube. Then with monetization on the amount of views you get, which is roughly $10,000 per million views, you can make a nice paycheck. A lot of the people doing this, in particular Simeon Boikov (aka Aussie Cossack) became semi-famous in the movement but their egos would usually cause them to mess up and breach the terms of YouTube and eventually get banned. I think that moron is still in hiding at the Russian Embassy after he live-streamed himself assaulting an elderly man and a warrant issued for his arrest, probably delusionally thinking he is a now a political prisoner like Julian Assange.

Avi Yemini, another Melbourne based citizen journalist, is an expert at "grifting". I found some videos by commentator Tom Tanuki and Lucky Lance online demonstrating his attempts at convincing his followers to donate their hard-earned cash to him through a dodgy news outlet called "Rebel News" based in Canada with Yemini being the Australian correspondent. His campaigns to "fight the COVID fines" which took in hundreds of thousands of dollars, never required a lawyer to that amount, but pocketed the rest which is a standard scam in the grifting business.

On Australia Day a couple of years ago, he made a video live from the back of a police van claiming he was under arrest. This has been a main stable for Avi as he rocks up every year on that day to offend protesters and get footage of their sometimes awkward and hostile reactions. The police know him all too well and this year, similar to previous years, he was given nothing more than a move-on order. The police consider him more like a pest and usually put him in their van, dropping him off a few blocks away with that same move-on order again and the warning that if he comes back, he will be charged with disturbing the peace.

"I'm now in the back of a police car and I've been arrested for what they alledge is a breach of the peace. The breach was that I attended the so-called invasion day to report and do my job. I came with my federal accreditation from the government"

(It was actually a press pass only valid in Canberra for interviewing foreign political visitors)

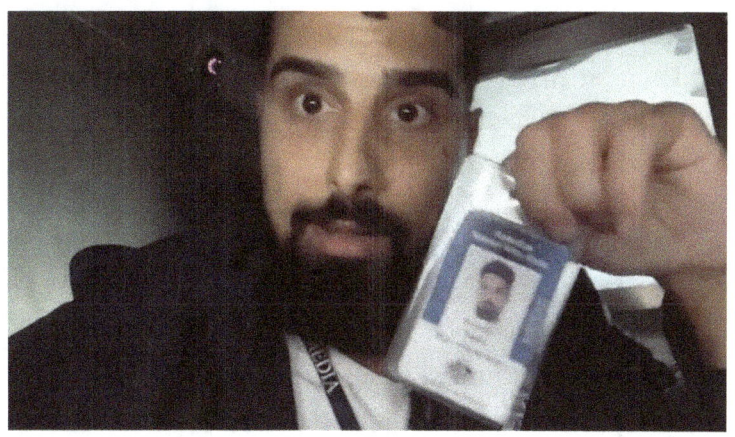

"I'm now being driven to an undisclosed location and I don't know if I am going to be charged. But I need your help. Please go to "rebelnews.com/freeavi" right now to help secure my freedom. I've got my gun lawyer Madeline on the case right now fighting to secure my freedom so I can go back and do my job...If you can cover the cost of my legal battle that I'm in right now then please donate"

The problem lies with the fact that someone monitoring the Rebel News website noticed this footage had gone online less than forty minutes after he live streamed himself in the police van. So in reality this page had gone up after the police had released him with the move-on order and Rebel News was promoting this "Free Avi" donation page to fight his legal battle when there wasn't a case to begin with.

But there was a much more damning nail in the coffin for

Avi and Rebel News. A Twitter user scanned the logo of the "Avi Yemini Arrested" banner and discovered the the image in question was made over five hours before according to the meta-data electronic fingerprint and created in North America by a member of Rebel News. That proves undoubtedly that Yemini and his Rebel News cohorts conspired hours before the arrest (which they knew happens every year on that day when he shows up at the rally) to create a donation page to crowdfund for a nonexisting legal case. If this wasn't true then why haven't Rebel News or Avi himself attempted to sue Tom Tanuki or Lucky Lance for breaking the story and exposing the scam?

After getting to know Lucky Lance a bit longer and seeing how much work he was doing behind the scenes to expose these scammers, we decided to meet in person and let the scamming/anti-everything movement know I had defected "live" on social media. I had been somewhat undercover during the previous month and assisting detectives with information about protests via the Telegram app but it was now time to declare my alliance with Lance.

We met up at Mordialoc Pier where I was fishing and he offered to drive me home. We made a stop on the way to film a video enlightening the movement that I had changed sides. We chose to do it out the front of a Masonic Centre just to rub salt into the wounds as the anti-everything movement and their Qanon theories believed the Masons are demon worshippers ready to make a New World Order and put in "the great reset" to reestablish society through a huge depopulation created through the "COVID hoax". There is no "New World Order" trying to take over the world, what benefit they have in reality of doing that? The wealth of the world and all underneath relies on everyone not so wealthy trying to their climb their way upwards, so to "eliminate them" would solve nothing! Anyway, to explore the NWO and Qanon theories would be another book in itself, one I am happy to explore, but I would rather focus on my journey first before trying to fully explain that deep dark rabbit hole in further detail.

Lance & myself out front of a Masonic Centre

We did a few takes and then I appeared on camera with Lance and was proud to do it, but the following weeks I received threats which I would consider ranging from extreme violent attacks to death. They were always worded in a pseudo-threatening way with a fake account but I passed them on to the police. One threat said "Pliers, Blowtorch" and I replied "Talking about the movies Pulp Fiction or Chopper?". I have never and will never back down from a bully or a threat.

In the following protests after I left the movement the level of violence against police increased significantly. I was watching a livestream from Rukshan Fernando (aka. The Real Rukshan) and there was a stand-off with police as they had kettled a crowd of hundreds. Suddenly the police line was broken by techniques I wrote about in my anti-police book and almost simultaneously on Avi Yemini's live stream from a different location, the same thing happened. I was hoping that part of my book was not shared by my cousin but I am fairly certain the Peacemakers probably got given a copy from her partner Sam Cowley.

I saw a police officer knocked out cold with a coward punch from one of the protesters as they broke the line, another one taken down with some sort of MMA (Mixed Martial Arts) grappling move and flares being thrown at the police. This was a far sight different than when I was involved and I was stunned as these pretend citizen journalists would edit the footage later on to make it look like police were the aggressors when they would retaliate with pepper spray and rubber bullets to keep the mob of many thousands from full-on rioting.

My new mission was my alliance with Lance in taking down these fraudsters, so I would save all the protest live videos and go through them and identify who was doing what and would pass my findings onto detectives. Matt Lawson, the leader who ran away like a coward when I was with him and about to challenge the cops, complained the police were way out of line and showed Avi his injuries from the rubber bullets on his stomach which were nothing more than getting shot with a paintball gun.

In August of 2021 Monica Smit, leader of the political movement "Reignite Democracy Australia", filmed her arrest in her car as she was taken into custody for a few weeks on charges of incitement. Lucky Lance was over the moon and did a video praising Victoria Police and pouring an expensive bottle of champagne over his head while laughing like a maniac. He couldn't mention her name on camera because she and others had multiple intervention orders against him, which in time were all eventually thrown out of court. It was again sad to see such deliberate misuse of a court system just to silence a critic of grifting and Lance has probably had the most intervention orders in Australian history.

Except here is the catch, Lucky Lance has the time and he fights every single order against himself and has never lost in court with any final intervention orders ever granted. The consequence of lying in your statement and having your case heard and the discovery of your false accusations is...nothing! And during those months and years when Monica Smit, Avi Yemini and many others have filed them against Lance, he has had to remain silent while they bagged him and try to humiliate him publicly online. My hat goes off to you Lance!

Lucky Lance successful in court yet again fighting fraudulent Intervention Orders

3

The Age

As the protests continued I mentally had to back away completely and by November of that year, I felt I had moved on from that unfortunate time in my life. I was now fully vaxxed and had moved back to St Kilda where two good friends of mine from the "Blackie" (Blackburn Hotel) were now also living. Emma had been there for a while and Brad, my pool teacher from Blackburn moved across the street from me about a month after I did. We called ourselves the "Three Amigos of St Kilda" and Brad, who had always struggled to find money during COVID thanks to his hospitality job, was back at work and appeared to have found a new true home. The three of us would hang out a few times a week and usually have more than a few drinks. He would often come over to my apartment and we would sit there and chat about life until he would fall asleep.

I was still in regular contact with Lance and he mentioned a journalist from "The Age" wanted to reach out and talk to me about my time in the anti-everything cult. I didn't want to revisit that part of my life. I had moved on as well as being offered a placement the following year doing my Masters Degree at the Australian Institute of Music. Lance subtly kept suggesting it might be a good idea to at least talk to the reporter and if an article is printed about my journey, it might help others get out of that movement. Around December I agreed, although still slightly reluctantly and Lance put me in contact with Rachael Dexter from "The Age" newspaper.

Over a few phone calls, I divulged my anti-lockdown/anti-everything journey and eventually in January we met in person to film some supplementary video footage for the online version of her upcoming article. I was still only a few weeks out of recovering from catching the COVID-omicron variation so my health was okay but certainly not in good summer health. I caught COVID at a New Year's Eve party and had been double vaxxed so I was saved from the life-threatening aspect of it, but it was pure hell for a few days. I was bedridden with an incredible fever made worse by weather temperatures being around the mid-thirties celsius and I had to crawl to get to the bathroom. Emma, Brad and my parents would drop food at my gate while my body was in shocking agony all over. After a few days it passed fairly quickly and the symptoms were that of a mild cold.

The filming segment for The Age article was a very emotional and draining few hours re-visiting my story in front of a camera with Rachael asking me sometimes very difficult questions, but I braved through it with honesty and the article was set for release a few weeks later, just as the uprising in Canberra of sovereign citizen protesters was at its peak against the government and it's COVID response in general. Here are some extracts from that article:

Falling into the 'freedom' movement ... and getting out
By Rachael Dexter (February 13, 2022)

At the height of Melbourne's anti-lockdown protests, Ash Jackson was a familiar face. Front and centre of screaming crowds, she dutifully waved flags, clashed with police and was arrested several times. For almost a year she was consumed as a follower of the 'freedom' movement – entire days were spent online, reading and watching anti-government videos and posts on encrypted social media apps, becoming increasingly paranoid, angry and obsessed. Jackson turned up on the news more than once after being arrested and shunned by family and friends. But now she's out.

About eight months after leaving the movement, she still can't believe the grip it had on her life. Jackson says if you had asked her a year ago where she might be in 2022, she would have said in a concentration camp for the unvaccinated or engaged in an insurrection after a communist takeover. "I was thinking by this time ... that we'd have an underground movement with weaponry," says the 48-year-old.

In her small Melbourne apartment, Jackson brings up a YouTube video on her television. It's a Channel 7 report from February 20, 2021, the day hundreds of protesters marched to the Shrine of Remembrance and ended up being corralled by police at Fawkner Park, where dozens were arrested. Amid the angry mobs, Jackson points to herself. That day, while attending the protest, she was arrested after marching up to a group of police to conduct a "citizen's arrest" of the officers for "crimes against humanity". "I was so brainwashed" she says as she watches the chaotic scenes, shaking her head.

The 'freedom' movement, initially centred around anti-lockdown and anti-vaccine sentiment, saw protesters take to the streets, particularly in Melbourne, every weekend for almost two years to reject COVID health measures. Last year, as lockdowns lifted, the movement's leaders shifted their attention to vaccine mandates. This year protesters have descended on Canberra, including on Saturday, talking about everything from the dangers of vaccination to QAnon-adjacent theories about paedophiles within the Australian government.

At the extreme edges are those who claim they are willing, as "sovereign citizens", to launch a full government takeover – violent or otherwise. In his latest annual threat assessment, delivered this week, the boss of Australia's counter-espionage agency ASIO, Mike Burgess, highlights growing concern about online radicalisation during the pandemic, noting vaccine mandates and lockdowns had fuelled extremism that is not "specifically left or right-wing". "More time in those online environments — without some of the circuit breakers of everyday life, like family and community engagement, school and work — created more extremists," he wrote.

Just before the emergence of COVID-19 in early 2020, Jackson was working part-time as a musician; composing music for productions, gigging around Melbourne's suburbs in cover bands and teaching guitar. Victoria's initial six-week lockdown drove her out of work. She had no real social interaction for more than two months. At home, scrolling on her phone, she found anti-lockdown groups starting to call out what they saw as overly harsh measures from an increasingly dangerous police state. "I stumbled across some things on the internet, and I was like 'Oh this makes sense, I don't want to be locked down'," she says.

She can't remember the specific video or post that first touched her conspiracy nerve, but she became a big fan of influencers such as Monica Smit of Reignite Democracy Australia – a lobby group backing Craig Kelly and the United Australia Party – Smit's partner, podcaster Morgan Jonas and Avi Yemini from Canada-based right-wing commentary website Rebel News. "I was slowly finding myself getting brainwashed," Jackson says. "I kept looking into conspiracy theories, including QAnon. I started rooting for Donald Trump, which was ridiculous. Being trans ... he's not very favourable to us." Once a born-again Christian, Jackson had left her faith over a decade earlier, ousted from her church for coming out as transgender. It was a deeply wounding experience she still has trouble talking about. "I've sort of been a little bit of a loner [since]," she says. "I found a bit of community in the anti-lockdown movement."

She became a regular on the front line at Melbourne's anti-lockdown rallies, coming onto police's radar for disseminating a handbook on how to thwart officers at protests. "I got sucked in big time to the point where I was doing ... very dodgy illegal stuff that I'm ashamed of now, but at the time I thought it was justified," she says. She's visibly distressed about the abuse she hurled at police on the front line. "I gave them so much shit, I called them every name under the sun," she says.

It was her experience with Victoria Police that planted the seed for her escape. In late May last year, at her last 'freedom' protest, she was encouraged by other protesters to throw herself in front of police after receiving a move-on notice. Police arrested her, while she says the others ran away. "I was kind of thinking, 'Where the hell are my friends?'" she recalls. "They all just buggered off and left me. "I was confused ... so I didn't give the police a hard time at all. And they said, 'Look, we're going to give you a move-on because you've been so cooperative'."

The following week Jackson was arrested at home and taken in for questioning over her role in the protests and the anti-police booklet circulating online. When the formal interview was over, she says officers spoke to her candidly about their life, their families, and how difficult it had been working on the front line during the pandemic, showing sympathy for her struggles with her gender and mental health. "I realised, 'These aren't the Gestapo or anything ... I had it all wrong'. "I had tears when I was just talking candidly with them just saying, 'God how have I f---ed my life up like this?'

Police didn't lay charges that day and offered Jackson a lift home. "I said, 'No, actually, I wouldn't mind walking. I need to think about my life'." Jackson went home and fell into a deep, days-long depressive spell, during which she self-harmed. By this point, she had lost ties with her extended family, had a criminal record, and felt she had been manipulated. Around this time she found others online who had grown skeptical of the movement and had begun questioning the extraordinary amounts of money being raised. This and follow-up welfare visits by the police were the final impetus for her to leave the 'freedom' movement. "The weight that came off my shoulders instantly – it was unbelievable," she says. "If I didn't leave, I would have probably ended up in some sort of psych ward or something. When you believe strongly in something and that the police are coming for you, the government's coming for you, you're going to get sent to a concentration camp. "I used to be in my apartment and I'd have the door barricaded with a couch and tables. I'd booby-trapped the windows. "It was consuming and eating me away. Just destroying my soul and my friendships – I lost a lot of friends." "And so it looks like people aren't just passive consumers of information. They're working towards finding stuff that makes sense to them or makes sense of the world for them."

Jackson says she is now getting her life back on track. She's recently moved house for a fresh start after a long period of recovery living with her parents and this week is going back to university to study for a masters degree in music. She recently recovered from COVID-19 too, a mild case she attributes to now being vaccinated.

She becomes emotional when she talks about her extended family, who welcomed her back at Christmas. "The biggest moving part for me was seeing my nieces," she says. "I didn't see my nieces for like eight months and I love my nieces. And just seeing them again was amazing." "I was expecting I was going to have to spend [Christmas] by myself and I got a call from my brother the day before and he said, 'You're more than welcome. What's in the past is in the past, and we're glad that you're safe and that you're out of that."

Ash still keeps an eye on the movement, which was responsible for a fire at Old Parliament House in December and has now set up a permanent camp at the Canberra Showgrounds with leaders claiming to stay put until the government is "cleaned out". Amid calls for an end to vaccine mandates and vaccine passports are speeches about the "paedophile cabal" by leaders who have repeatedly called for MPs to be hanged. Last week convoy leader James Greer, who raised almost $200,000 in crowdfunding for the protest, was arrested after police found a loaded rifle and ammunition in his car at the protest campground. "It's so different to what it was even a year ago," says Jackson. "I can fully see some sort of domestic terrorist thing happen." She believes most people will "have to hit rock bottom themselves" to leave the movement and hopes her story helps others. "I still care about some of these people, you know? I hope they can get out."

Rachael did a sensational job on the article treating it with clear solid facts and compassion and it was met with a positive response except for the anti-everything movement. In particular, Monica Smit who wrote an online press release on the Reignite Democracy website playing down my role in the movement and trying to defend the negative vibe of the story towards her organisation, but she was positive in her overall comments of my character but never referred to me as any pronoun, just "Ash". She said I was welcome back to the

Reignite family anytime. But I had other things on my mind, a few days earlier I had been to a funeral and my soul was feeling desperately crushed by the loss of one of my best friends. Brad was gone!

I remember him sitting on my couch a week earlier saying "Ash you are a real true friend"... I had known him for about five years after we met with his girlfriend Liz playing pool at the Blackburn Hotel. I had only just started playing pool and enjoying the solitude of practicing by myself and occasionally asking a stranger for a game. Brad and Liz were playing on the adjacent pool table and he asked where I played competition and for which club. Little did I know that was him joking with a deadpan face because I was shit at the game. He gave me some coaching that day in exchange for shouting him a couple of beers. Over the next few weeks we would bump into each other and he introduced me around to the locals. He worked at a restaurant as the manager about a street away and he and Liz both became good friends over time, even standing strong beside me when I transitioned again years later.

A couple of weeks earlier on Australia Day 2022 I saw him sitting on the steps of the local tram stop near where we lived in St Kilda and he was crying in pain. He had been going through extreme bouts of agony in his left shoulder for several months and claimed he needed surgery to fix damaged nerves but because of COVID, all elective surgery was on hold. I offered to take him across the road to the local clinic just to get seen because I was very concerned but he refused and I had to help him walk back to his home opposite my place. A few hours later he called me and asked if I could go to the local supermarket and get him a few things and so I happily obliged not knowing it would be the last time I would see him alive as he greeted me at his back gate to collect. Emma had spoken with him a few hours later that night and we thought it odd the next day when we left him messages to hang out after work but received no response.

The following morning I was at my parents and got a call from Liz asking me to check on Brad because she also hadn't heard from him either. I was in the car with my mum getting a lift back home when Emma called me saying she was at Brad's and the landlord was there about to open the room he was renting. All I heard in the confusion was Emma saying "Come here quick, I think he's hurt or might have passed". As my mum dropped me off I jogged as best I could through the pouring rain to Brad's place just as an ambulance and police were arriving. Emma was in the foyer and I asked what was happening and she said she didn't know because they wouldn't let her see him.

An officer came to us to inform us that he had passed away and I burst into tears as me and Emma hugged. We sat with the police as the paramedics asked us questions about him and his general health. My heart was crushed and I called my mum who had gone to see if Liz to was alright or even aware of what was happening. The sergeant informed LIz over the phone that Brad had passed and I broke down again, this time more concerned for Liz as she had just lost her mother to cancer a couple of years earlier and now her boyfriend too.

The rest of that day and the following days were a blur of tears mixed with heavy drinking and trying to comprehend how a forty-seven-year-old could die from a heart attack. The funeral was a disgraceful attempt by his family that he barely knew and it included no friends being asked to participate. We were the ones who knew him best. We were his family. I still feel like I had no real closure but as I sit here and write this with tears streaming down my face, I want to say thank you to you Brad for your friendship and the thousands of laughs and good times we shared. I wish you could have lived to know that I ended up a few months later working in hospitality just like you. Thanks for letting me win a game of pool occasionally too. Farewell, my friend...

4

The Project

After the article in "The Age" came out I received several offers from other media outlets including ABC "The Drum" as well as radio, but one in a pile of messages was from Channel 10's prime-time award-winning current affairs show called "The Project". I wanted to get this message out to as many people as possible, so that became my first preference as I replied and had a phone call with one of the show's producers. We agreed that doing a special segment would convey my journey with much more justice instead of sitting at the desk doing a live interview, in addition it would allow double the amount of air-time so the next day I was at channel 10 in South Yarra at the Como building where I met with the producer Georgia.

Because COVID was still around and gaining traction again from the Omicron variant, I was not allowed to get my makeup done at the studio so my dear friend Laura did it. The lighting was quite intense and overall I looked pretty ordinary even though she did do a sensational job on my face. The camera crew was absolutely miles ahead of anyone I had worked with at Oz Fish TV and Georgia was an absolutely lovely and compassionate producer knowing this was going to be a very hard thing for me to do.

As I touched up my makeup and sat down the host Waleed Aly came in and we had a brief chat. He was an A-grade celebrity, a Logie Award winner and a very intelligent and humble guy. We sat as he interviewed me for a good ninety minutes and then off-camera for about half an hour, sharing guitar talk as he was also a very talented musician as well as a journalist. I was not paid for anything by any media outlet including The Age or The Project and I would have refused even if anything was offered.

People needed to know there was a way out of conspiracy theories and cult-like organisations and I felt Waleed asked the right questions and added the right commentary to explain both sides of the anti-lockdown movement and the general public's response to them. After thanking and saying goodbye to Waleed, the remaining three of us (Georgia, the cameraman and myself) departed for a quick lunch then off to the city to film some supplementary footage at Parliament House and eventually back at my apartment.

As the days passed my anticipation grew and I was starting to wonder after a whole week if they had abandoned the story. Georgia apologised for the delay but they needed that extra time to get the segment perfect. She said if I wanted to pursue any other media that was fine so I did a radio interview on the ABC a few hours before "The Project" was about to put my journey live on national television.

Then just after 7pm, alone in my apartment with the television on and a nice cold beer in my hand, I awaited my television premiere. It was Wednesday the 23rd of February 2022 and the story was about to air. It was about my pain. About my loneliness and desperation to find a community that cared for me. Part of me wanted to turn it off and lock myself in my room for the next few weeks until it all passed. I didn't want the attention. I didn't want to be recognised. But the message was too important to walk away from.

I could see myself on the box sitting across from the host Waleed. It was a surreal moment. I was so sad. I guess that made sense because my best friend had passed away a fortnight before. I was still a mess trying to cope day by day with my devastation. There I was on screen talking about the past two years of my life...

Ash: When you go to a protest, it's kind of like being at a rock concert. The adrenaline is unbelievable. We thought it was like the beginning of Nazi Germany again and Victoria Police were the Gestapo. I truly believed that we we're headed towards a police state.

Waleed: It's a crazy concept, but one Ash says she truly believed in because at the time she had nothing else to believe in. She had lost her job, her freedom and over time, her will to live. How lonely would you say you were feeling at that time?

Ash: At points, probably suicidal.

Waleed: Ash supported lockdowns at first but confronted with a tidal wave of misinformation online, she quickly changed her mind.

Ash: I was sitting there sixteen hours a day, just on the internet, doing my research and I started believing it. At the time I just thought I was fighting for the freedom of Australia.

Waleed: Ash, who is transgender, says being part of the freedom movement made her feel accepted. What did you like about these people?

Ash: There is a lot of love in that community, a lot of misinformation. which I didn't realise at the time. People coming up to me, giving me hugs and adding me on Facebook. I felt like I was important. But when you're reading that much information and you're at the protest calling the police every name and then you're barricading your door because you think the police and ASIO are after you, it becomes stressful. It just consumes your whole life in a very unhealthy way.

Waleed: Ash says her family didn't support her views, so she cut ties with them. She saw the other protesters as her brothers and sisters until they abandoned her one day.

Ash: The police were say 100 metres away walking towards us.

I go, OK, we're going to stand our ground. What they're doing isn't ethical and I'm marching with my flag and I turn around and they all had buggered off.

Waleed: All the other protesters?

Ash: Yeah. including one of the leaders.

Waleed: Ash decided to cooperate with the police. They didn't arrest her, just told her to go home.

Ash: The police rock up at my door a few days later, six of them. Normally I'd get up and say "F--- Off" and slam the door and stuff and I kind of gave it up. They were treating me very well. They're like "We've got families too, and we don't necessarily want to be at the protest, but our job is law enforcement".

Waleed: Over the following weeks, police dropped over to Ash's place a few times.

Ash: I was blown away that they'd come just to check up on me. These people are kind of treating me better than some of the leaders of the protest movement did.

Waleed: Ash says the fog around her head began to clear. Her feelings changed from anger to guilt.

Ash: I consider myself that I was brainwashed, but a lot of that was also my fault. The way I treated authorities and the things I wrote on the internet, I feel really ashamed, and I want to put this part of my life to bed.

Waleed: Since she's left the movement, Ash has reconciled with her family, been vaccinated and started a Masters Degree in music. Her true passion. But putting this chapter of her life behind her hasn't been easy. Ash says she's received death threats from protesters. Do you feel scared?

Ash: I feel cautious, not scared. I'm more concerned for my family.

Waleed: So in what way?

Ash: I hope they don't, you know, take it out on them in any way. I own this. This is my mistake. Part of me is glad I went through it because I probably would have necked myself if I didn't find some sort of community, but yeah there's just so much shame involved. I find it hard to smile to be honest.

Waleed: Do you think you'll ever be able to forgive yourself or move passed that feeling of shame?

Ash: Yeah things are looking more positive for me. As much as I know that what some of the protesters are doing isn't 100% right, I still care about some of them.

Waleed: Do you think that those of us in society looking at the protesters and kind of being dismissive and scornful of them, do you think we're making a mistake?

Ash: Yeah, I think there needs to be a little bit more understanding that they're human beings. Right or wrong, that's what they believe, and they deserve a little bit more compassion.

STUDIO COMMENTARY AFTER THE SEGMENT:
Gosh, that desire to be connected and to be part of something is such a strong desire. And you can see how quickly it happens. You think of your phone, and how quickly the algorithm changes, and then you start getting fed all the same information, and before you know it, that is the truth, that you're the truth because you're not seeing anything else. So it was a matter of weeks. Yeah. It was extraordinary how fast that happened. I've heard a lot about the idea that it's like a rock concert. Like looking at the Canberra convoy that feels like a festival almost. Like, they're sharing food, they're taking care of each other, they're singing songs together, there's this other side to it that most of us don't understand. Yeah and I feel that the point that's so important is the point at the end about listening to each other and I think when you stand and yell at people, either way, no one's going to take being yelled at and say "Yeah, good point". So it's a matter of listening to each other. She just wanted people to listen to each other.

I got calls from friends and family saying how well it was presented and I felt proud that I dared to follow through that far, all the while knowing the backlash was going to be severe. I got recognised several times on the street over the next few weeks but it was all positive comments, except the trolls online that would amount to thousands of negative comments, yet not one of them about what I did, it was all about what I was. I screen-captured some of their comments and forwarded them to their friends list so maybe some of them received a nice little dose of karma...

Michael David Morris
He looks just like the Biden Health Minister 😉
Like Reply 1 w

Tasos Papadopoulos
Michael David Morris Twin sister...or should I say brother? 😄
Like Reply 1 w

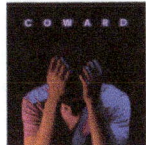
Troy Tempest
wow just looked at pic un relised who it is seen her before a shill she/he is a man in diffrent guises on here but the face u cannot change

Angela Cadwallen
Not even going to give them a click. This bloke obviously has all sorts of issues and would be the last person I would be taking advice from in regards to the freedom movement. I was in a cult once, the Catholic Church, I think I can tell the difference!
Like Reply 1 w

Karyn Shalagin
She?
Like Reply 1 w

Des Tan
Karyn Shalagin it's a trans
Like Reply 1 w

Mel Ann · Follow
I find it pretty alarming the amount of people that have to resort to insults about gender in the comments.

So much for 'freedom'

These sorts of derogatory remarks are absolutely not necessary.

You can pick and pull a part so many contradictory statements in this interview and make your point without resorting to petty insults.

Your lack of ability to do so just demonstrates how incapable you are of articulating your point.

2y Like Reply   13

Robert Troisi
I'd be interested to know if Ash was paid for this so-called interview. They slipped in how bad these protests are, promoted the police, and pushed vaccinations. That so-called interviewer should stick to comedy.

2y Like Reply   16

Oskar Bock
Main stream media always interview the hot chick's. They're taking advantage of her beauty..

2y Like Reply   6

> **Alex Nómad**
> **Oskar Bock** her???
>
> 2y Like Reply   4
>
>> **H-j Anderson**
>> **Alex Nómad** - exactly what I was thinking too
>>
>> 2y Like Reply

Marjie Spies
I watched the interview, this person used to spend I think it was 16 hours a day watching conspiracy videos!
Disgusting, biased "journalism". Absolute BS and exploitation of her. But I'm sure she got a nice paycheck from channel 10.

2y Like Reply   20

5

Aftermath

Speaking of assholes, Rukshan Fernando (aka Real Rukshan) being a very ordinary citizen journalist, did a video reply to my segment on The Project and he was trying to bait me as the troll he is. So I rose to the occasion and took the bait to reply to his lack of journalistic integrity and research to do a live online video with Lucky Lance and tore Rukshan a new one. Here is that extract courtesy of Lance:

Ash: So the real Rukshan, I'm giving him the courtesy of calling him by his professional name, which he didn't give me in his video. He just kept referring to me as a "certain individual" a "certain person" and never named me once. So my integrity is a lot higher than his and so I'll be referring to him as "Rukshan" or "Real Rukshan" because I'm not going to stoop that low.

Lance: He doesn't have any integrity so you're wrong there. He doesn't have any level of integrity.

Ash: That's what I mean, but I have some.

Lance: Yes, you do.

Ash: So I want to reply to a couple of things that he said and also there were a couple of important questions that some of his followers asked. One of his followers asked how much I paid, I'm a shill and I'm doing this for money. I can tell you now that I got paid nothing. I wasn't offered anything from any of the media that I've done since The Age, the ABC, The Project, whatever. And even if they did offer me money, I wouldn't have taken it ... Okay, I got paid on last Friday, and I have that much left after my bills. (showing on screen around $30 cash) *So yeah, I need it... but my integrity, I couldn't do it.*

Lance: So categorically, you weren't paid, you didn't ask to be paid, you weren't offered to be paid and making money was a furthest thing from your mind. You just wanted to tell your story, your experience in the movement. So that's that debate.

Ash: Yeah, I think that's nipped in the butt now. They can go and contact Channel 10 or whatever they need to do and they'll get the same answer. One of the things Rukshan said, again, I bring up on referring to his name, not calling him a certain individual, is he kept saying that I was distributing at protests a radical extremist pamphlet which is made up. I've never done such a thing. The only thing remotely even close to that concept would be I was writing a novel set in the dystopian future and there was a chapter on counter tactics against police. That kind of shows you the lies that he says. His followers just believe it straight away. That's not the case at all. I've never distributed anything at any protest except giving people hugs.

Lance: Well, I've met a lot of journalists in the last two years. And what I've been shocked when it comes to journalists, I've rang journalists and said, I've got a story for you. This person in the movement has done this, which is, whether it's fraudulent, illegal, whatever it is. And every time they're like, oh, now we can't go to print on that if we can't verify it. And I think I've got really good proof. They're like, now we need more verification, we can't go to print without stronger verification of the facts. And I had a big shock. I was quite shocked. I was like, wow, I didn't know that so many people in media had this type of integrity. Because some people in the media do tell lies sometimes. They have about me in the past. But anyway, I was shocked that in general, all the journalists that I've spoken to on the phone in the last two years, their level of integrity is high. Whereas with Rukshan, he's not a journalist, he's heard third hand from a "cooker" that you were handing out pamphlets. And he just puts that into his story as fact. Now, one very important fact, I don't know if you were gonna say this, but if Rukshan was a journalist, we wouldn't be having this conversation because you would be putting a complaint to the press council and they would force him to make a retraction. Right?

Ash: Another comment he said that if he felt and he said it's quite evident that I've been exploited by Waleed and The Project and I'm a depressed individual with all these problems and whatever he was saying. I wasn't exploited at all. They treated me well and were very compassionate with the story and

I thought they did quite a balanced story showing compassion on both sides.

Lance: Exactly. It was simply a person giving an honest story of your experience in the movement. You just told your story. You had nothing to hide. You had nothing to gain. You had no motivation to embellish or exaggerate. It was just a simple interview of you telling your story and you were quite nice. You didn't use rude words or you didn't insult anyone. You just simply gave your take on your experience in the movement, that's all that was. And Rukshan has come out and tried to make it out to be something else.

Ash: But that should show you something as well by me doing that, the bi-product of it is that they're worried because they know that movement is in its last stages. It's starting to unravel, they're starting to implode, turn on each other and create new angles. They know the game is up. We're going back to our normal society slowly, but we're getting there. They expected us to already be in a police state and when I was in that brainwashed cult of idealism, I thought the same thing. This is the last point anyway. I've copped many thousands of comments and I've read a few of them. To be honest, I'm quite thick-skinned. And of course, when you read it, it's not enjoyable, but it kind of gives me a chuckle because every single one of them is attacking me personally about being transgender. They're so insecure about their movement and cause that they can't discredit anything that I said on The Project or anything in print, so I thought that was quite interesting and quite telling of that movement because they're quite right-winged and they're not fans of the LGBT community.

Lance: Yeah, well, he's pretty quiet on acknowledging the fact that there are Nazis in the protest. He likes to avoid that.

Ash: Even though he had a picture with good old Neil Erickson. Well, that's the thing, it has been infiltrated. When I was in it, there was no talk like that and no "Peacemakers". They were just sort of a thing starting up with Nick Patterson and after I left I noticed the violence did increase quite significantly to the point where they're smashing police officers out and throwing flares and all that stuff. It kind of makes me wonder because there's just so much evidence against their narrative. Do they truly think that the worldwide media, all the governments, all the leaders, absolutely billions of us have conspired just to make COVID up? Even when I was brainwashed I kind of thought "Oh okay maybe COVID might be a more severe version of the flu or more contagious" but I've had it...you've had it. I can tell you it's frickin real it hits you like a freight train and if you aren't vaxxed then that freight train might continue to derail...

FINAL THOUGHTS:

I have been fairly harsh on occasion to some of the people in the anti-everything movement and sometimes probably a bit too harsh. A documentary called "Battleground Melbourne" came out around this time, documenting the protest movement and the hard-line enforced by Victoria Police during the lockdown. Initially, I didn't even watch it all and jumped on the bandwagon and bagged it out, but a year or so after its release I sat down with an open mind and empathy and, although I don't agree with some of the opinions, I must say that Topher Field, the director, did make a good documentation of things that happened while we were locked down. I wrote to him apologising for my strong words and also praising him on a job well done and he appreciated that.

Around the middle of 2022, the television show "Sixty Minutes" reported on the neo-nazi movement in Australia with an undercover reporter infiltrating it over several months with a hidden camera. It was interesting to see that some of those faces were people I had seen marching with the anti-lockdown protesters . I couldn't believe it how police protected them during their rallies where they did the nazi salute at an anti-transgender protest, a protest organised by the same anti-lockdown movement. And then counter-protesters got arrested for disturbing the peace while these scumbags get an escort from the cops to and from their cars.

As far as my involvement went I was done with everything

regarding protesting, but I also was pleased that I had accomplished something that may help others and myself, it was time to ignore the haters and move on. It was a time of terrible turmoil in my life, and by writing this story I feel it has helped me to let it go…

www.ingramcontent.com/pod-product-compliance
Lightning Source LLC
Chambersburg PA
CBHW072107290426
44110CB00014B/1859